OLD TESTAMENT MIRACLES

The Supernatural Lies Outside the Natural
System of Causation

OLD TESTAMENT MIRACLES

The Supernatural Lies Outside the Natural System of Causation

Compiled by Eugene Carvalho

TABLE OF CONTENTS

PURPOSE AND ACKNOWLEDGEMENTS

The infallible Word of God for faith and conduct informs us that the Holy Spirit gives gifts to men and women of the Body of Christ. It states: "the gifts edify the body for the building up of the saints" (Eph. 4:12). I hope the talents and gifts the Lord has given me will be a blessing to someone else through the reading of this compilation.

I am grateful for the love from all family members, especially my wife Mercedes Carvalho. I am also grateful for the knowledge, wisdom and love of many pastors, teachers, and saints that the Lord has used to bless me. Lastly, I must not forget a special thank you to my dear friend Kathryn Regan for proofreading this material.

Chapter One

SUPERNATURAL DEFINED

Faith is the currency of the Kingdom of God. The Bible says, "So faith comes from hearing, and hearing by the word of Christ" (Ro. 10:17).[1] Reading about supernatural miracles in the Bible will certainly build our faith. Miracles are supernatural events which abound in the Old Testament scriptures. Allow me to define the terms: supernatural, supernatural qualities, supernatural realm, and spiritual for you. "**Supernatural** – Pertaining to that which falls outside of or cannot be accounted for by the laws of the physical universe. **Supernatural qualities** – Attributes not found in human beings or in nature apart from God's special working. **Supernatural realm** – That which lies outside the boundaries of the physical universe or of the natural system of causation."[2] "**Spiritual** - (pneumatikos, 'spiritual,' from pneuma, 'spirit'): Endowed with the attributes of spirit. Any being made in the image of God who is a Spirit (Joh. 4:24.), and thus having the nature of spirit, is a spiritual being. (1) Spiritual hosts of wickedness (Eph. 6:12), in distinction from beings clothed in 'flesh and blood' — the devil and his angels. This use of the word has reference to nature, essence, and not to character or moral quality. God, angels, man, devil, demons are in essence spiritual. The groundwork and faculties of their rational and moral being are the same. This limited use of the word in the New Testament has its adverb equivalent in Re. 11:8, 'which (the great and

---

[1] All Scripture quotations, unless otherwise noted, are from the *New American Standard Bible*.

[2] Millard J. Erickson, *The Concise Dictionary of Christian Theology* (Grand Rapids: Baker Books, 1986), 193.

wicked city) spiritually is called Sodom.' As the comprehensive term moral includes immoral, so spiritual includes unspiritual and all that pertains to spirit. (2) With the above exception, 'spiritual' in the New Testament signifies moral, not physical antithesis: an essence springing from the Spirit of God and imparted to the spirit of man. Hence, spiritual in this sense always presupposes the infusion of the Holy Spirit to quicken, and inform. It is opposed (a) to sarkikos, 'fleshly' (1Cor. 3:1), men of the flesh and not of the spirit; (b) to psuchikos, 'natural,' man in whom the pneuma, 'spirit,' is over-ridden, because of the Fall, by psuche, the principle of the animal life, 'soul'; hence, the unrenewed man, unspiritual, alienated from the life of God (1Cor. 2:14; 2 Pet. 2:12; Jd. 1:10). (c) to natural, meaning physical, '.... sown a natural body; .... raised a spiritual body' (1Cor. 15:44). (3) In the New Testament and general use 'spiritual' thus indicates man regenerated, indwelt, enlightened, endued, empowered, guided by the Holy Spirit; conformed to the will of God, having the mind of Christ, living in and led by the Spirit. The spiritual man is a new creation born from above (Ro. 8:6; 1 Cor. 2:15; 3:1; 14:37; Col. 1:9; 1 Pet. 2:5). (4) Ecclesiastically used of things sacred or religious, as spiritual authority, spiritual assembly, spiritual office."[3]

Throughout this compilation I will be discussing supernatural miracles that are mentioned in the Old Testament. I am sure they will stir you up and build your faith.

---

[3] *International Standard Bible Encyclopedia* , accessed from Online Bible Software (2009 Edition), 26 November, 2010

MIRACLES IN THE OLD TESTAMENT

The Creation – The Bible says: "In the beginning God created the heavens and the earth. The earth was formless and void, and darkness was over the surface of the deep, and the Spirit of God was moving over the surface of the waters. Then God said, 'Let there be light'; and there was light. God saw that the light was good; and God separated the light from the darkness. God called the light day, and the darkness He called night. And there was evening and there was morning, one day. Then God said, 'Let there be an expanse in the midst of the waters, and let it separate the waters from the waters.' God made the expanse, and separated the waters which were below the expanse from the waters which were above the expanse; and it was so. God called the expanse heaven. And there was evening and there was morning, a second day. Then God said, 'Let the waters below the heavens be gathered into one place, and let the dry land appear'; and it was so. God called the dry land earth, and the gathering of the waters He called seas; and God saw that it was good. Then God said, 'Let the earth sprout vegetation: plants yielding seed, and fruit trees on the earth bearing fruit after their kind with seed in them'; and it was so. The earth brought forth vegetation, plants yielding seed after their kind, and trees bearing fruit with seed in them, after their kind; and God saw that it was good. There was evening and there was morning, a third day. Then God said, 'Let there be lights in the expanse of the heavens to separate the day from the night, and let them be for signs and for seasons and for days and years; and let them be for lights in the expanse of the heavens to give light on the earth'; and it was so. God made the two great lights, the greater light to govern the day, and the lesser light to govern the night; He made the stars also. God placed them in the expanse of the heavens to give light on the earth, and to govern the day and the night, and to separate the light from the darkness; and God saw that it was good. There was evening and there was morning, a fourth day. Then God said, 'Let the waters teem with swarms of living creatures, and let birds fly above the earth in the open expanse of the heavens.' God created the great sea monsters and every living creature that moves, with which the waters swarmed after their kind, and every winged bird after its kind; and God saw that it was good. God blessed them, saying, 'Be fruitful and multiply, and fill the waters in the seas, and let birds multiply on the earth.' There was evening and there was morning, a fifth day. Then God said, 'Let the earth bring forth living creatures after their kind: cattle and creeping things and beasts of the earth after their kind'; and it was so. God made the beasts of the earth after their kind, and the cattle after their kind, and everything that creeps on the ground after its kind; and God saw that it was good. Then God said, 'Let Us make man in Our image, according to Our likeness; and let them rule over the fish of the sea and over the birds of the sky and over the cattle and over all the earth, and over every creeping thing that creeps on the earth.' God created man in His own image, in the image of God He created him; male and female He created them. God blessed them; and God said to them, 'Be fruitful and multiply, and fill the earth, and subdue it; and rule over the fish of the sea and over the birds of the sky and over every living thing that moves on the earth.' Then God said, 'Behold, I have given you every plant yielding seed that is on the surface of all the earth, and every tree which has fruit yielding seed; it shall be food for you; and to every beast of the earth and to every bird of the sky and to everything that moves on the earth which has life, I have given every green plant for food'; and it was so. God saw all that He had made, and behold, it was very good. And there was evening and there was morning, the sixth day" (Gen. 1:1-31).

The Flood / The Flood Subsides - "Then the Lord said to Noah, 'Enter the ark, you and all your household, for you alone I have seen to be righteous before Me in this time. You shall take with you of every clean animal by sevens, a male and his female; and of the animals that are not clean two, a male and his female; also of the birds of the sky, by sevens, male and female, to keep offspring alive on the face of all the earth. 'For after seven more days, I will send rain on the earth forty days and forty nights; and I will blot out from the face of the land every living thing that I have made.' Noah did according to all that the Lord had commanded him. Now Noah was six hundred years old when the flood of water came upon the earth. Then Noah and his sons and his wife and his sons' wives with him entered the ark because of the water of the flood. Of clean animals and animals that are not clean and birds and everything that creeps on the ground, there went into the ark to Noah by twos, male and female, as God had commanded Noah. It came about after the seven days that the water of the flood came upon the earth. In the six hundredth year of Noah's life, in the second month, on the seventeenth day of the month, on the same day all the fountains of the great deep burst open and the floodgates of the sky were opened. The rain fell upon the earth for forty days and forty nights. On the very same day Noah and Shem and Ham and Japheth, the sons of Noah, and Noah's wife and the three wives of his sons with them, entered the ark, they and every beast after its kind, and all the cattle after their kind, and every creeping thing that creeps on the earth after its kind, and every bird after its kind, all sorts of birds. So they went into the ark to Noah, by twos of all flesh in which was the breath of life. Those that entered, male and female of all flesh, entered as God had commanded him; and the Lord closed it behind him. Then the flood came upon the earth for forty days, and the water increased and lifted up the ark, so that it rose above the earth. The water prevailed and increased greatly upon the earth, and the ark floated on the surface of the water. The water prevailed more and more upon the earth, so that all the high mountains everywhere under the heavens were covered. The water prevailed fifteen cubits higher, and the mountains were covered. All flesh that moved on the earth perished, birds and cattle and beasts and every swarming thing that swarms upon the earth, and all mankind; of all that was on the dry land, all in whose nostrils was the breath of the spirit of life, died. Thus He blotted out every living thing that was upon the face of the land, from man to animals to creeping things and to birds of the sky, and they were blotted out from the earth; and only Noah was left, together with those that were with him in the ark. The water prevailed upon the earth one hundred and fifty days. But God remembered Noah and all the beasts and all the cattle that were with him in the ark; and God caused a wind to pass over the earth, and the water subsided. Also the fountains of the deep and the floodgates of the sky were closed, and the rain from the sky was restrained; and the water receded steadily from the earth, and at the end of one hundred and fifty days the water decreased. In the seventh month, on the seventeenth day of the month, the ark rested upon the mountains of Ararat. The water decreased steadily until the tenth month; in the tenth month, on the first day of the month, the tops of the mountains became visible. Then it came about at the end of forty days, that Noah opened the window of the ark which he had made; and he sent out a raven, and it flew here and there until the water was dried up from the earth. Then he sent out a dove from him, to see if the water was abated from the face of the land; but the dove found no resting place for the sole of her foot, so she returned to him into the ark, for the water was on the surface of all the earth. Then he put out his hand and took her, and brought her into the ark to himself. So he waited yet another seven days; and again he sent out the dove from the ark. The dove came to him toward evening, and behold, in her beak was a freshly picked olive leaf. So Noah knew that the water was abated from the earth. Then he waited yet another seven days, and sent out the dove; but she did not return to him again. Now it came about in the six hundred and first year, in the first month, on the first of the month, the water was dried up from the earth. Then Noah removed the covering of the ark, and looked, and behold, the surface of the ground was dried up. In the second month, on the twenty-seventh day of the month, the earth was dry. Then God spoke to Noah, saying, 'Go out of the ark, you and your wife and your sons and your sons' wives with you. Bring out with you every living thing of all flesh that is with you, birds and animals and every creeping thing that creeps on the earth, that they may breed abundantly on the earth, and be fruitful and multiply on the earth.' So Noah went out, and his sons and his wife and his sons' wives with him. Every beast, every creeping thing, and every bird, everything that moves on the earth, went out by their families from the ark. Then Noah built an altar to the Lord, and took of every clean animal and of every clean bird and offered burnt offerings on the altar. The Lord smelled the soothing aroma; and the Lord said to Himself, 'I will never again curse the ground on account of man, for the intent of man's heart is evil from his youth; and I will never again destroy every living thing, as I have done. While the earth remains, Seedtime and harvest, and cold and heat, and summer and winter, and day and night shall not cease'" (Gen. 7, 8).

Universal Language, Babel, Confusion - "Now the whole earth used the same language and the same words. It came about as they journeyed east, that they found a plain in the land of Shinar and settled there. They said to one another, 'Come, let us make bricks and burn them thoroughly.' And they used brick for stone, and they used tar for mortar. They said, 'Come, let us build for ourselves a city, and a tower whose top will reach into heaven, and let us make for ourselves a name, otherwise we will be scattered abroad over the face of the whole earth.' The Lord came down to see the city and the tower which the sons of men had built. The Lord said, 'Behold, they are one people, and they all have the same language. And this is what they began to do, and now nothing which they purpose to do will be impossible for them. Come, let us go down and there confuse their language, so that they will not understand one another's speech.' So the Lord scattered them abroad from there over the face of the whole earth; and they stopped building the city.

Therefore its name was called Babel, because there the Lord confused the language of the whole earth; and from there the Lord scattered them abroad over the face of the whole earth" (Gen. 11:1-9).

A Flaming Torch on Abraham's Sacrifice – "It came about when the sun had set, that it was very dark, and behold, there appeared a smoking oven and a flaming torch which passed between these pieces. On that day the Lord made a covenant with Abram, saying, 'To your descendants I have given this land, From the river of Egypt as far as the great river, the river Euphrates:
the Kenite and the Kenizzite and the Kadmonite and the Hittite and the Perizzite and the Rephaim and the Amorite and the Canaanite and the Girgashite and the Jebusite'" (Gen. 15:17-21).

The Conception of Isaac – "Then God said to Abraham, 'As for Sarai your wife, you shall not call her name Sarai, but Sarah shall be her name. I will bless her, and indeed I will give you a son by her. Then I will bless her, and she shall be a mother of nations; kings of peoples will come from her.' Then Abraham fell on his face and laughed, and said in his heart, 'Will a child be born to a man one hundred years old? And will Sarah, who is ninety years old, bear a child?' And Abraham said to God, 'Oh that Ishmael might live before You!'
But God said, 'No, but Sarah your wife will bear you a son, and you shall call his name Isaac; and I will establish My covenant with him for an everlasting covenant for his descendants after him. As for Ishmael, I have heard you; behold, I will bless him, and will make him fruitful and will multiply him exceedingly. He shall become the father of twelve princes, and I will make him a great nation. But My covenant I will

establish with Isaac, whom Sarah will bear to you at this season next year.' When He finished talking with him, God went up from Abraham" (Gen. 17:15-22).

The Doom of Sodom – "Now the two angels came to Sodom in the evening as Lot was sitting in the gate of Sodom. When Lot saw them, he rose to meet them and bowed down with his face to the ground. And he said, 'Now behold, my lords, please turn aside into your servant's house, and spend the night, and wash your feet; then you may rise early and go on your way.' They said however, 'No, but we shall spend the night in the square.' Yet he urged them strongly, so they turned aside to him and entered his house; and he prepared a feast for them, and baked unleavened bread, and they ate. Before they lay down, the men of the city, the men of Sodom, surrounded the house, both young and old, all the people from every quarter; and they called to Lot and said to him, 'Where are the men who came to you tonight? Bring them out to us that we may have relations with them.' But Lot went out to them at the doorway, and shut the door behind him, and said, 'Please, my brothers, do not act wickedly. Now behold, I have two daughters who have not had relations with man; please let me bring them out to you, and do to them whatever you like; only do nothing to these men, inasmuch as they have come under the shelter of my roof.' But they said, 'Stand aside.' Furthermore, they said, 'This one came in as an alien, and already he is acting like a judge; now we will treat you worse than them.' So they pressed hard against Lot and came near to break the door. But the men reached out their hands and brought Lot into the house with them, and shut the door. They struck the men who were at the doorway of the house with blindness, both small and great, so that they wearied themselves trying to find the doorway. Then the two men said to Lot, 'Who else have you here? A son-in-law, and your sons, and your daughters, and whomever you have in the city, bring them out of the place; for we are about to destroy this place, because their outcry has become so great before the Lord that the Lord has sent us to destroy it.' Lot went out and spoke to his sons-in-law, who were to marry his daughters, and said, 'Up, get out of this place, for the Lord will destroy the city.' But he appeared to his sons-in-law to be jesting. When morning dawned, the angels urged Lot, saying, 'Up, take your wife and your two daughters who are here, or you will be swept away in the punishment of the city.' But he hesitated. So the men seized his hand and the hand of his wife and the hands of his two daughters, for the compassion of the Lord was upon him; and they brought him out, and put him outside the city. When they had brought them outside, one said, 'Escape for your life! Do not look behind you, and do not stay anywhere in the valley; escape to the mountains, or you will be swept away.' But Lot said to them, 'Oh no, my lords! Now behold, your servant has found favor in your sight, and you have magnified your lovingkindness, which you have shown me by saving my life; but I cannot escape to the mountains, for the disaster will overtake me and I will die; now behold, this town is near enough to flee to, and it is small. Please, let me escape there (is it not small?) that my life may be saved.' He said to him, 'Behold, I grant you this request also, not to overthrow the town of which you have spoken. Hurry, escape there, for I cannot do anything until you arrive there.' Therefore the name of the town was called Zoar. The sun had risen over the earth when Lot came to Zoar.

Then the Lord rained on Sodom and Gomorrah brimstone and fire from the Lord out of heaven, and He overthrew those cities, and all the valley, and all the inhabitants of the cities, and what grew on the ground. But his wife, from behind him, looked back, and she became a pillar of salt. Now Abraham arose early in the morning and went to the place where he had stood before the Lord; and he looked down toward Sodom and Gomorrah, and toward all the land of the valley, and he saw, and behold, the smoke of the land ascended like the smoke of a furnace. Thus it came about, when God destroyed the cities of the valley, that God remembered Abraham, and sent Lot out of the midst of the overthrow, when He overthrew the cities in which Lot lived. Lot went up from Zoar, and stayed in the mountains and his two daughters with him; for he was afraid to stay in Zoar; and he stayed in a cave, he and his two daughters. Then the firstborn said to the younger, 'Our father is old, and there is not a man on earth to come in to us after the manner of the earth. Come, let us make our father drink wine, and let us lie with him that we may preserve our family through our father.' So they made their father drink wine that night, and the firstborn went in and lay with her father; and he did not know when she lay down or when she arose. On the following day, the firstborn said to the younger, 'Behold, I lay last night with my father; let us make him drink wine tonight also; then you go in and lie with him, that we may preserve our family through our father.' So they made their father drink wine that night also, and the younger arose and lay with him; and he did not know when she lay down or when she arose. Thus both the daughters of Lot were with child by their father. The firstborn bore a son, and called his name Moab; he is the father of the Moabites to this day.

As for the younger, she also bore a son, and called his name Ben-ammi; he is the father of the sons of Ammon to this day" (Gen. 19).

Lot's Wife Became a Pillar of Salt – "The sun had risen over the earth when Lot came to Zoar. Then the Lord rained on Sodom and Gomorrah brimstone and fire from the Lord out of heaven, and He overthrew those cities, and the entire valley, and all the inhabitants of the cities, and what grew on the ground. But his wife, from behind him, looked back, and she became a pillar of salt" (Gen. 19:23-26).

Healing of Abimelech's Household - "So Abimelech arose early in the morning and called all his servants and told all these things in their hearing; and the men were greatly frightened. Then Abimelech called Abraham and said to him, 'What have you done to us? And how have I sinned against you, that you have brought on me and on my kingdom a great sin? You have done to me things that ought not to be done.' And Abimelech said to Abraham, 'What have you encountered, that you have done this thing?' Abraham said, 'Because I thought, surely there is no fear of God in this place, and they will kill me because of my wife. Besides, she actually is my sister, the daughter of my father, but not the daughter of my mother, and she became my wife; and it came about, when God caused me to wander from my father's house, that I said to her, "This is the kindness which you will show to me: everywhere we go, say of me, 'He is my brother.'"' Abimelech then took sheep and oxen and male and female servants, and gave them to Abraham, and restored his wife Sarah to him. Abimelech said, 'Behold, my land is before you; settle wherever you please.' To Sarah he said, 'Behold, I have given your brother a thousand pieces of silver; behold, it is your vindication before all who are with you, and before all men you are cleared.' Abraham prayed to God, and God healed Abimelech and his wife and his maids, so that they bore children. For the Lord had closed fast all the wombs of the household of Abimelech because of Sarah, Abraham's wife" (Gen. 20:8-18).

God Opens Hagar's Eyes – "When the water in the skin was used up, she left the boy under one of the bushes. Then she went and sat down opposite him, about a bowshot away, for she said, 'Do not let me see the boy die.' And she sat opposite him, and lifted up her voice and wept. God heard the lad crying; and the angel of God called to Hagar from heaven and said to her, 'What is the matter with you, Hagar? Do not fear, for God has heard the voice of the lad where he is. Arise, lift up the lad, and hold him by the hand, for I will make a great nation of him.' Then God opened her eyes and she saw a well of water; and she went and filled the skin with water and gave the lad a drink" (Gen. 21:15-19).

The Conception of Jacob and Esau – "Now these are the records of the generations of Isaac, Abraham's son: Abraham became the father of Isaac; and Isaac was forty years old when he took Rebekah, the daughter of Bethuel the Aramean of Paddan-aram, the sister of Laban the Aramean, to be his wife. Isaac prayed to the Lord on behalf of his wife, because she was barren; and the Lord answered him and Rebekah his wife conceived. But the children struggled together within her; and she said, 'If it is so, why then am I this way?' So she went to inquire of the Lord. The Lord said to her, 'Two nations are in your womb; and two peoples will be separated from your body; and one people shall be stronger than the other; And the older shall serve the younger'" (Gen. 25:19-23).

Rachel's Womb is Opened – "Then God remembered Rachel, and God gave heed to her and opened her womb. So she conceived and bore a son and said, 'God has taken away my reproach.' She named him Joseph, saying, 'May the Lord give me another son'" (Gen. 30:22-24).

The Burning Bush – "Now Moses was pasturing the flock of Jethro his father-in-law, the priest of Midian; and he led the flock to the west side of the wilderness and came to Horeb, the mountain of God. The angel of the Lord appeared to him in a blazing fire from the midst of a bush; and he looked, and behold, the bush was burning with fire, yet the bush was not consumed. So Moses said, 'I must turn aside now and see this marvelous sight, why the bush is not burned up.' When the Lord saw that he turned aside to look, God called to him from the midst of the bush and said, 'Moses, Moses!' And he said, 'Here I am.' Then He said, 'Do not come near here; remove your sandals from your feet, for the place on which you are standing is holy ground.' He said also, 'I am the God of your father, the God of Abraham, the God of Isaac, and the God of Jacob.' Then Moses hid his face, for he was afraid to look at God" (Ex. 3:1-6).

Moses's Given Powers – "Then Moses said, 'What if they will not believe me or listen to what I say? For they may say, "The Lord has not appeared to you."' The Lord said to him, 'What is that in your hand?' And he said, 'A staff.' Then He said, 'Throw it on the ground.' So he threw it on the ground, and it became a serpent; and Moses fled from it. But the Lord said to Moses, 'Stretch out your hand and grasp it by its tail' — so he stretched out his hand and caught it, and it became a staff in his hand — 'that they may believe that the Lord, the God of their fathers, the God of Abraham, the God of Isaac, and the God of Jacob, has appeared to you'" (Ex. 4:1-5).

Moses's Leprosy – "The Lord furthermore said to him, 'Now put your hand into your bosom.' So he put his hand into his bosom, and when he took it out, behold, his hand was leprous like snow. Then He said, 'Put your hand into your bosom again.' So he put his hand into his bosom again, and when he took it out of his bosom, behold, it was restored like the rest of his flesh. 'If they will not believe you or heed the witness of the first sign, they may believe the witness of the last sign. But if they will not believe even these two signs or heed what you say, then you shall take some water from the Nile and pour it on the dry ground; and the water which you take from the Nile will become blood on the dry ground'" (Ex. 4:6-9).

The Ten Plagues of Egypt

In the book of Exodus, Pharaoh refused to let the Hebrew people leave Egypt. The ten plagues were a divine demonstration of power and disapproval intended to sway Pharaoh to "let God's people go." They are listed below in chronological order.

1. Water to Blood – "Then the Lord said to Moses, 'Say to Aaron, "Take your staff and stretch out your hand over the waters of Egypt, over their rivers, over their streams, and over their pools, and over all their reservoirs of water, that they may become blood; and there will be blood throughout all the land of Egypt, both in vessels of wood and in vessels of stone'"'" (Ex. 7:19).

2. Frogs – "'But if you refuse to let them go, behold, I will smite your whole territory with frogs. The Nile will swarm with frogs, which will come up and go into your house and into your bedroom and on your bed, and into the houses of your servants and on your people, and into your ovens and into your kneading bowls. So the frogs will come up on you and your people and all your servants'" (Ex. 8:2-4).

3. Lice – "Then the Lord said to Moses, 'Say to Aaron, "Stretch out your staff and strike the dust of the earth, that it may become gnats through all the land of Egypt'"'" (Ex. 8:16).

4. Flies – "'For if you do not let My people go, behold, I will send swarms of insects on you and on your servants and on your people and into your houses; and the houses of the Egyptians will be full of swarms of insects, and also the ground on which they dwell'" (Ex. 8:21).

5. Livestock Diseased – "'Behold, the hand of the Lord will come with a very severe pestilence on your livestock which are in the field, on the horses, on the donkeys, on the camels, on the herds, and on the flocks'" (Ex. 9:3).

6. Boils – "Then the Lord said to Moses and Aaron, 'Take for yourselves handfuls of soot from a kiln, and let Moses throw it toward the sky in the sight of Pharaoh'" (Ex. 9:8).

7. Thunder and Hail – "'Behold, about this time tomorrow, I will send a very heavy hail, such as has not been seen in Egypt from the day it was founded until now'" (Ex. 9:18).

8. Locust – "'For if you refuse to let My people go, behold, tomorrow I will bring locusts into your territory. They shall cover the surface of the land, so that no one will be able to see the land. They will also eat the rest of what has escaped—what is left to you from the hail—and they will eat every tree which sprouts for you out of the field'" (Ex. 10:4-5).

9. Darkness – "Then the Lord said to Moses, 'Stretch out your hand toward the sky, that there may be darkness over the land of Egypt, even a darkness which may be felt.' So Moses stretched out his hand toward the sky, and there was thick darkness in all the land of Egypt for three days" (Ex. 10:21-22).

10. Death of Firstborn – "Moses said, 'Thus says the Lord, about midnight I am going out into the midst of Egypt, and all the firstborn in the land of Egypt shall die, from the firstborn of the Pharaoh who sits on his throne, even to the firstborn of the slave girl who is behind the millstones; all the firstborn of the cattle as well'" (Ex. 11:4-5).

God Leads the People – "Now when Pharaoh had let the people go, God did not lead them by the way of the land of the Philistines, even though it was near; for God said, 'The people might change their minds when they see war, and return to Egypt.' Hence God led the people around by the way of the wilderness to the Red Sea; and the sons of Israel went up in martial array from the land of Egypt. Moses took the bones of Joseph with him, for he had made the sons of Israel solemnly swear, saying, 'God will surely take care of you, and you shall carry my bones from here with you.' Then they set out from Succoth and camped in Etham on the edge of the wilderness. The Lord was going before them in a pillar of cloud by day to lead them on the way, and in a pillar of fire by night to give them light, that they might travel by day and by night" (Ex. 13:17-22).

The Sea is Divided – "Then Moses stretched out his hand over the sea; and the Lord swept the sea back by a strong east wind all night and turned the sea into dry land, so the waters were divided. The sons of Israel went through the midst of the sea on the dry land, and the waters were like a wall to them on their right hand and on their left. Then the Egyptians took up the pursuit, and all Pharaoh's horses, his chariots and his horsemen went in after them into the midst of the sea. At the morning watch, the Lord looked down on the army of the Egyptians through the pillar of fire and cloud and brought the army of the Egyptians into confusion" (Ex. 14:21-24).

Pharaoh and his Army are Destroyed – "He caused their chariot wheels to swerve, and He made them drive with difficulty; so the Egyptians said, 'Let us flee from Israel, for the Lord is fighting for them against the Egyptians.' Then the Lord said to Moses, 'Stretch out your hand over the sea so that the waters may come back over the Egyptians, over their chariots and their horsemen.' So Moses stretched out his hand over the sea, and the sea returned to its normal state at daybreak, while the Egyptians were fleeing right into it; then the Lord overthrew the Egyptians in the midst of the sea. The waters returned and covered the chariots and the horsemen, even Pharaoh's entire army that had gone into the sea after them; not even one of them remained. But the sons of Israel walked on dry land through the midst of the sea, and the waters were like a wall to them on their right hand and on their left" (Ex. 14:25- 29).

Waters Became Sweet – "Then Moses led Israel from the Red Sea, and they went out into the wilderness of Shur; and they went three days in the wilderness and found no water. When they came to Marah, they could not drink the waters of Marah, for they were bitter; therefore it was named Marah. So the people grumbled at Moses, saying, 'What shall we drink?' Then he cried out to the Lord, and the Lord showed him a tree; and he threw it into the waters, and the waters became sweet. There He made for them a statute and regulation, and there He tested them. And He said, 'If you will give earnest heed to the voice of the Lord your God, and do what is right in His sight, and give ear to His commandments, and keep all His statutes, I will put none of the diseases on you which I have put on the Egyptians; for I, the Lord, am your healer.' Then they came to Elim where there were twelve springs of water and seventy date palms, and they camped there beside the waters" (Ex. 15:22-27).

The Lord Provides Manna – "Then the Lord said to Moses, 'Behold, I will rain bread from heaven for you;

and the people shall go out and gather a day's portion every day, that I may test them, whether or not they will walk in My instruction. On the sixth day, when they prepare what they bring in, it will be twice as much as they gather daily.' So Moses and Aaron said to all the sons of Israel, 'At evening you will know that the Lord has brought you out of the land of Egypt; and in the morning you will see the glory of the Lord, for He hears your grumblings against the Lord; and what are we, that you grumble against us'" (Ex. 16:4-7)?

The Lord Provides Meat – "So it came about at evening that the quails came up and covered the camp, and in the morning there was a layer of dew around the camp" (Ex. 16:13).

Victory: Against Amalek – "Then Amalek came and fought against Israel at Rephidim. So Moses said to Joshua, 'Choose men for us and go out, fight against Amalek. Tomorrow I will station myself on the top of the hill with the staff of God in my hand.' Joshua did as Moses told him, and fought against Amalek; and Moses, Aaron, and Hur went up to the top of the hill.
So it came about when Moses held his hand up, that Israel prevailed, and when he let his hand down, Amalek prevailed. But Moses' hands were heavy. Then they took a stone and put it under him, and he sat on it; and Aaron and Hur supported his hands, one on one side and one on the other. Thus his hands were steady until the sun set. So Joshua overwhelmed Amalek and his people with the edge of the sword" (Ex. 17:8-13).

Moses Face Shines – "It came about when Moses was coming down from Mount Sinai (and the two tablets of the testimony were in Moses' hand as he was coming down from the mountain), that Moses did not know that the skin of his face shone because of his speaking with Him. So when Aaron and all the sons of Israel saw Moses, behold, the skin of his face shone, and they were afraid to come near him. Then Moses called to them, and Aaron and all the rulers in the congregation returned to him; and Moses spoke to them. Afterward all the sons of Israel came near and he commanded them to do everything that the Lord had spoken to him on Mount Sinai. When Moses had finished speaking with them, he put a veil over his face. But whenever Moses went in before the Lord to speak with Him, he would take off the veil until he came out; and whenever he came out and spoke to the sons of Israel what he had been commanded, the sons of Israel would see the face of Moses, that the skin of Moses' face shone. So Moses would replace the veil over his face until he went in to speak with Him" (Ex. 34:29-35).

Water in the Rock – "Then the Lord said to Moses, 'Pass before the people and take with you some of the elders of Israel; and take in your hand your staff with which you struck the Nile, and go. Behold, I will stand before you there on the rock at Horeb; and you shall strike the rock, and water will come out of it, that the people may drink.' And Moses did so in the sight of the elders of Israel. He named the place Massah and Meribah because of the quarrel of the sons of Israel, and because they tested the Lord, saying, 'Is the Lord among us, or not?'" (Ex. 17:5-7).

Thundering and Lightning Flashes – "So it came about on the third day, when it was morning, that there were thunder and lightning flashes and a thick cloud upon the mountain and a very loud trumpet sound, so that all the people who were in the camp trembled. And Moses brought the people out of the camp to meet God, and they stood at the foot of the mountain. Now Mount Sinai was all in smoke because the Lord descended upon it in fire; and its smoke ascended like the smoke of a furnace, and the whole mountain quaked violently. When the sound of the trumpet grew louder and louder, Moses spoke and God answered him with thunder. The Lord came down on Mount Sinai, to the top of the mountain; and the Lord called Moses to the top of the mountain, and Moses went up" (Ex. 19:16-20).

Miriam's was Leprous – "So the anger of the Lord burned against them and He departed. But when the cloud had withdrawn from over the tent, behold, Miriam was leprous, as white as snow. As Aaron turned toward Miriam, behold, she was leprous. Then Aaron said to Moses, 'Oh, my lord, I beg you, do not account this sin to us, in which we have acted foolishly and in which we have sinned. Oh, do not let her be like one dead, whose flesh is half eaten away when he comes from his mother's womb!' Moses cried out to the Lord, saying, 'O God, heal her, I pray!' But the Lord said to Moses, 'If her father had but spit in her face, would she not bear her shame for seven days? Let her be shut up for seven days outside the camp, and afterward she may be received again.' So Miriam was shut up outside the camp for seven days, and the people did not move on until Miriam was received again" (Nu. 12:9-15).

Judgment: The Fire of the Lord – "Now the people became like those who complain of adversity in the hearing of the Lord; and when the Lord heard it, His anger was kindled, and the fire of the Lord burned among them and consumed some of the outskirts of the camp. The people therefore cried out to Moses, and Moses prayed to the Lord and the fire died out. So the name of that place was called Taberah, because the fire of the Lord burned among them" (Nu. 11:1-3).

Judgment: Korah's Rebellion – "As he finished speaking all these words, the ground that was under them split open; and the earth opened its mouth and swallowed them up, and their households, and all the men who belonged to Korah with their possessions. So they and all that belonged to them went down alive to Sheol; and the earth closed over them, and they perished from the midst of the assembly. All Israel who were around them fled at their outcry, for they said, 'The earth may swallow us up!' Fire also came forth from the Lord and consumed the two hundred and fifty men who were offering the incense" (Nu. 16:31-35).

Murmuring and Plague – "But on the next day all the congregation of the sons of Israel grumbled against Moses and Aaron, saying, 'You are the ones who have caused the death of the Lord's people.' It came about, however, when the congregation had assembled against Moses and Aaron, that they turned toward the tent of meeting, and behold, the cloud covered it and the glory of the Lord appeared. Then Moses and Aaron came to the front of the tent of meeting, and the Lord spoke to Moses, saying, 'Get away from among this congregation, that I may consume them instantly.' Then they fell on their faces. Moses said to Aaron, 'Take your censer and put in it fire from the altar, and lay incense on it; then bring it quickly to the congregation and make atonement for them, for wrath has gone forth from the Lord, the plague has begun!' Then Aaron took it as Moses had spoken, and ran into the midst of the assembly, for behold, the plague had begun among the people. So he put on the incense and made atonement for the people. He took his stand between the dead and the living, so that the plague was checked. But those who died by the plague were 14,700, besides those who died on account of Korah. Then Aaron returned to Moses at the doorway of the tent of meeting, for the plague had been checked" (Nu. 16:41-50).

Aaron's Rod Buds – "Then the Lord spoke to Moses, saying, 'Speak to the sons of Israel, and get from them a rod for each father's household: twelve rods, from all their leaders according to their fathers' households. You shall write each name on his rod, and write Aaron's name on the rod of Levi; for there is one rod for the head of each of their fathers' households. You shall then deposit them in the tent of meeting in front of the testimony, where I meet with you. It will come about that the rod of the man whom I choose will sprout. Thus I will lessen from upon Myself the grumblings of the sons of Israel, who are grumbling against you.' Moses therefore spoke to the sons of Israel, and all their leaders gave him a rod apiece, for each leader according to their fathers' households, twelve rods, with the rod of Aaron among their rods. So Moses deposited the rods before the Lord in the tent of the testimony. Now on the next day Moses went into the tent of the testimony; and behold, the rod of Aaron for the house of Levi had sprouted and put forth buds and produced blossoms, and it bore ripe almonds. Moses then brought out all the rods from the presence of the Lord to all the sons of Israel; and they looked, and each man took his rod. But the Lord said to Moses, 'Put back the rod of Aaron before the testimony to be kept as a sign against the rebels, that you may put an end to their grumblings against Me, so that they will not die.' Thus Moses did; just as the Lord had commanded him, so he did" (Nu. 17:1-11).

The Water of Meribah – "'Take the rod; and you and your brother Aaron assemble the congregation and speak to the rock before their eyes, that it may yield its water. You shall thus bring forth water for them out of the rock and let the congregation and their beasts drink.' So Moses took the rod from before the Lord, just as He had commanded him; and Moses and Aaron gathered the assembly before the rock. And he said to them, 'Listen now, you rebels; shall we bring forth water for you out of this rock?' Then Moses lifted up his hand and struck the rock twice with his rod; and water came forth abundantly, and the congregation and their beasts drank. But the Lord said to Moses and Aaron, 'Because you have not believed Me, to treat Me as holy in the sight of the sons of Israel, therefore you shall not bring this assembly into the land which I have given them.' Those were the waters of Meribah, because the sons of Israel contended with the Lord, and He proved Himself holy among them" (Nu. 20:8-13).

The Bronze Serpent – "The Lord sent fiery serpents among the people and they bit the people, so that many people of Israel died. So the people came to Moses and said, 'We have sinned, because we have spoken against the Lord and you; intercede with the Lord, that He may remove the serpents from us.' And Moses interceded for the people. Then the Lord said to

Moses, 'Make a fiery serpent, and set it on a standard; and it shall come about, that everyone who is bitten, when he looks at it, he will live.' And Moses made a bronze serpent and set it on the standard; and it came about, that if a serpent bit any man, when he looked to the bronze serpent, he lived" (Nu. 21:6-9).

The Sin of Nadab and Abihu – "Now Nadab and Abihu, the sons of Aaron, took their respective firepans, and after putting fire in them, placed incense on it and offered strange fire before the Lord, which He had not commanded them. And fire came out from the presence of the Lord and consumed them, and they died before the Lord. Then Moses said to Aaron, 'It is what the Lord spoke, saying, "By those who come near Me I will be treated as holy, And before all the people I will be honored.'" So Aaron, therefore, kept silent" (Lev. 10:1-3).

The Angel and Balaam – "So Balaam arose in the morning, and saddled his donkey and went with the leaders of Moab. But God was angry because he was going, and the angel of the Lord took his stand in the way as an adversary against him. Now he was riding on his donkey and his two servants were with him. When the donkey saw the angel of the Lord standing in the way with his drawn sword in his hand, the donkey turned off from the way and went into the field; but Balaam struck the donkey to turn her back into the way. Then the angel of the Lord stood in a narrow path of the vineyards, with a wall on this side and a wall on that side. When the donkey saw the angel of the Lord, she pressed herself to the wall and pressed Balaam's foot against the wall, so he struck her again. The angel of the Lord went further, and stood in a narrow place where there was no way to turn to the right hand or the left. When the donkey saw the angel of the Lord, she lay down under Balaam; so Balaam was angry and struck the donkey with his stick. And the Lord opened the mouth of the donkey, and she said to Balaam, 'What have I done to you, that you have struck me these three times?' Then Balaam said to the donkey, 'Because you have made a mockery of me! If there had been a sword in my hand, I would have killed you by now.' The donkey said to Balaam, 'Am I not your donkey on which you have ridden all your life to this day? Have I ever been accustomed to do so to you?' And he said, 'No'" (Nu. 22:21-30).

Israel Crosses the Jordan – "So when the people set out from their tents to cross the Jordan with the priests carrying the ark of the covenant before the people, and when those who carried the ark came into the Jordan, and the feet of the priests carrying the ark were dipped in the edge of the water (for the Jordan overflows all its banks all the days of harvest), the waters which were flowing down from above stood and rose up in one heap, a great distance away at Adam, the city that is beside Zarethan; and those which were flowing down toward the sea of the Arabah, the Salt Sea, were completely cut off. So the people crossed opposite Jericho. And the priests who carried the ark of the covenant of the Lord stood firm on dry ground in the middle of the Jordan while all Israel crossed on dry ground, until all the nation had finished crossing the Jordan" (Josh. 3:14-17).

The Conquest of Jericho – "Then on the seventh day they rose early at the dawning of the day and marched around the city in the same manner seven times; only on that day they marched around the city seven times.

At the seventh time, when the priests blew the trumpets, Joshua said to the people, 'Shout! For the Lord has given you the city. The city shall be under the ban, it and all that is in it belongs to the Lord; only Rahab the harlot and all who are with her in the house shall live, because she hid the messengers whom we sent. But as for you, only keep yourselves from the things under the ban, so that you do not covet them and take some of the things under the ban, and make the camp of Israel accursed and bring trouble on it. But all the silver and gold and articles of bronze and iron are holy to the Lord; they shall go into the treasury of the Lord.' So the people shouted, and priests blew the trumpets; and when the people heard the sound of the trumpet, the people shouted with a great shout and the wall fell down flat, so that the people went up into the city, every man straight ahead, and they took the city. They utterly destroyed everything in the city, both man and woman, young and old, and ox and sheep and donkey, with the edge of the sword" (Josh. 6:15-21).

Victory: The Camp of Midian – "When Gideon heard the account of the dream and its interpretation, he bowed in worship. He returned to the camp of Israel and said, 'Arise, for the Lord has given the camp of Midian into your hands.' He divided the 300 men into three companies, and he put trumpets and empty pitchers into the hands of all of them, with torches inside the pitchers. He said to them, 'Look at me and do likewise. And behold, when I come to the outskirts of the camp, do as I do. When I and all who are with me blow the trumpet, then you also blow the trumpets all around the camp and say, "For the Lord and for Gideon."' So Gideon and the hundred men who were with him came to the outskirts of the camp at the beginning of the middle watch, when they had just posted the watch; and they blew the trumpets and smashed the pitchers that were in their hands. When the three companies blew the trumpets and broke the pitchers, they held the torches in their left hands and the trumpets in their right hands for blowing, and cried, 'A sword for the Lord and for Gideon!' Each stood in his place around the camp; and all the army ran, crying out as they fled. When they blew 300 trumpets, the Lord set the sword of one against another even throughout the whole army; and the army fled as far as Beth-shittah toward Zererah, as far as the edge of Abel-meholah, by Tabbath. The men of Israel were summoned from Naphtali and Asher and all Manasseh, and they pursued Midian" (Jdg. 7:15-23).

Hailstones from Heaven – "Then the men of Gibeon sent word to Joshua to the camp at Gilgal, saying, 'Do not abandon your servants; come up to us quickly and save us and help us, for all the kings of the Amorites that live in the hill country have assembled against us.' So Joshua went up from Gilgal, he and all the people of war with him and all the valiant warriors. The Lord said to Joshua, 'Do not fear them, for I have given them into your hands; not one of them shall stand before you.' So Joshua came upon them suddenly by marching all night from Gilgal. And the Lord confounded them before Israel, and He slew them with a great slaughter at Gibeon, and pursued them by the way of the ascent of Beth-horon and struck them as far as Azekah and Makkedah. As they fled from before Israel, while they were at the descent of Beth-horon, the Lord threw large stones from heaven on them as far as Azekah, and they died; there were more who died from the hailstones than those whom the sons of Israel killed with the sword" (Josh. 10:6-11).

The Sun Stood Still and the Moon Stopped – "Then Joshua spoke to the Lord in the day when the Lord delivered up the Amorites before the sons of Israel, and he said in the sight of Israel, 'O sun, stand still at Gibeon, and O moon in the valley of Aijalon.' So the sun stood still, and the moon stopped, Until the nation avenged themselves of their enemies. Is it not written in the book of Jashar? And the sun stopped in the middle of the sky and did not hasten to go down for about a whole day. There was no day like that before it or after it, when the Lord listened to the voice of a man; for the Lord fought for Israel" (Josh. 10:12-14).

Sign of the Fleece – "Then Gideon said to God, 'If You will deliver Israel through me, as You have spoken, behold, I will put a fleece of wool on the threshing floor. If there is dew on the fleece only, and it is dry on all the ground, then I will know that You will deliver Israel through me, as You have spoken.' And it was so. When he arose early the next morning and squeezed the fleece, he drained the dew from the fleece, a bowl full of water. Then Gideon said to God, Do not let Your anger burn against me that I may speak once more; please let me make a test once more with the fleece, let it now be dry only on the fleece, and let there be dew on all the ground.' God did so that night; for it was dry only on the fleece, and dew was on all the ground" (Jdg. 6:36-40).

Samson's Tears a Young Goat – "Then Samson went down to Timnah with his father and mother, and came as far as the vineyards of Timnah; and behold, a young lion came roaring toward him. The Spirit of the Lord came upon him mightily, so that he tore him as one tears a young goat though he had nothing in his hand; but he did not tell his father or mother what he had done. So he went down and talked to the woman; and she looked good to Samson. When he returned later to take her, he turned aside to look at the carcass of the lion; and behold, a swarm of bees and honey were in the body of the lion. So he scraped the honey into his hands and went on, eating as he went. When he came to his father and mother, he gave some to them and they ate it; but he did not tell them that he had scraped the honey out of the body of the lion" (Jdg. 14:5-9).

Dagon Falls – "Now the Philistines took the ark of God and brought it from Ebenezer to Ashdod. Then the Philistines took the ark of God and brought it to the house of Dagon and set it by Dagon. When the Ashdodites arose early the next morning, behold, Dagon had fallen on his face to the ground before the ark of the Lord. So they took Dagon and set him in his place again. But when they arose early the next morning, behold, Dagon had fallen on his face to the ground before the ark of the Lord. And the head of Dagon and both the palms of his hands were cut off on the threshold; only the trunk of Dagon was left to him. Therefore neither the priests of Dagon nor all who enter Dagon's house tread on the threshold of Dagon in Ashdod to this day" (1 Sam. 5:1-5).

The Ark is Returned by Cows –"'Now then, get a new cart ready, with two cows that have calved and have never been yoked. Hitch the cows to the cart, but take their calves away and pen them up. Take the ark of the Lord and put it on the cart, and in a chest beside it put the gold objects you are sending back to him as a guilt offering. Send it on its way, but keep watching it. If it goes up to its own territory, toward Beth Shemesh, then the Lord has brought this great disaster on us. But if it does not, then we will know that it was not his hand that struck us but that it happened to us by chance.' So they did this. They took two such cows and hitched them to the cart and penned up their calves. They placed the ark of the Lord on the cart and along with it the chest containing the gold rats and the models of the tumors. Then the cows went straight up toward Beth Shemesh, keeping on the road and lowing all the way; they did not turn to the right or to the left. The rulers of the Philistines followed them as far as the border of Beth Shemesh. Now the people of Beth Shemesh were harvesting their wheat in the valley, and when they looked up and saw the ark, they rejoiced at the sight. The cart came to the field of Joshua of Beth Shemesh, and there it stopped beside a large rock. The people chopped up the wood of the cart and sacrificed the cows as a burnt offering to the Lord. The Levites took down the ark of the Lord, together with the chest containing the gold objects, and placed them on the large rock. On that day the people of Beth Shemesh offered burnt offerings and made sacrifices to the Lord. The five rulers of the Philistines saw all this and then returned that same day to Ekron" (1 Sam. 6:7-16).[4]

Men of Beth-shemesh Struck Down – "But God struck down some of the inhabitants of Beth Shemesh, putting seventy of them to death because they looked into the

---

[4] All Scripture quotations from this point forward, unless otherwise noted, are from the *New International Version*.

ark of the Lord. The people mourned because of the heavy blow the Lord had dealt them. And the people of Beth Shemesh asked, 'Who can stand in the presence of the Lord, this holy God? To whom will the ark go up from here?' Then they sent messengers to the people of Kiriath Jearim, saying, 'The Philistines have returned the ark of the Lord. Come down and take it up to your town'" (1 Sam. 6:19-21).

Thunder and Rain - "'But when you saw that Nahash king of the Ammonites was moving against you, you said to me, "No, we want a king to rule over us" — even though the Lord your God was your king. Now here is the king you have chosen, the one you asked for; see, the Lord has set a king over you. If you fear the Lord and serve and obey him and do not rebel against his commands, and if both you and the king who reigns over you follow the Lord your God — good! But if you do not obey the Lord, and if you rebel against his commands, his hand will be against you, as it was against your ancestors. Now then, stand still and see this great thing the Lord is about to do before your eyes! Is it not wheat harvest now? I will call on the Lord to send thunder and rain. And you will realize what an evil thing you did in the eyes of the Lord when you asked for a king.' Then Samuel called on the Lord, and that same day the Lord sent thunder and rain. So all the people stood in awe of the Lord and of Samuel" (1 Sam. 12:12-18).

God Struck Down Uzzah – "David again brought together all the able young men of Israel — thirty thousand. He and all his men went to Baalah in Judah to bring up from there the ark of God, which is called by the Name, the name of the Lord Almighty, who is enthroned between the cherubim on the ark. They set the ark of God on a new cart and brought it from the house of Abinadab, which was on the hill. Uzzah and Ahio, sons of Abinadab, were guiding the new cart with the ark of God on it, and Ahio was walking in front of it. David and all Israel were celebrating with all their might before the Lord, with castanets, harps, lyres, timbrels, sistrums and cymbals. When they came to the threshing floor of Nakon, Uzzah reached out and took hold of the ark of God, because the oxen stumbled. The Lord's anger burned against Uzzah because of his irreverent act; therefore God struck him down, and he died there beside the ark of God. Then David was angry because the Lord's wrath had broken out against Uzzah, and to this day that place is called Perez Uzzah. David was afraid of the Lord that day and said, 'How can the ark of the Lord ever come to me?' He was not willing to take the ark of the Lord to be with him in the City of David. Instead, he took it to the house of Obed-Edom the Gittite. The ark of the Lord remained in the house of Obed-Edom the Gittite for three months, and the Lord blessed him and his entire household" (2 Sam. 6:1-11).

Plague in Israel – "So the Lord sent a plague on Israel, and seventy thousand men of Israel fell dead. And God sent an angel to destroy Jerusalem. But as the angel was doing so, the Lord saw it and relented concerning the disaster and said to the angel who was destroying the people, 'Enough! Withdraw your hand.' The angel of the Lord was then standing at the threshing floor of Araunah the Jebusite. David looked up and saw the angel of the Lord standing between heaven and earth, with a drawn sword in his hand extended over Jerusalem. Then David and the elders, clothed in sackcloth, fell facedown. David said to God, 'Was it not I who ordered the fighting men to be counted? I, the shepherd, have sinned and done wrong. These are but sheep. What have they done? Lord my God, let your hand fall on me and my family, but do not let this plague remain on your people.' Then the angel of the Lord ordered Gad to tell David to go up and build an altar to the Lord on the threshing floor of Araunah the Jebusite. So David went up in obedience to the word that Gad had spoken in the name of the Lord. While Araunah was threshing wheat, he turned and saw the angel; his four sons who were with him hid themselves. Then David approached, and when Araunah looked and saw him, he left the threshing floor and bowed down before David with his face to the ground. David said to him, 'Let me have the site of your threshing floor so I can build an altar to the Lord, that the plague on the people may be stopped. Sell it to me at the full price.' Araunah said to David, 'Take it! Let my lord the king do whatever pleases him. Look, I will give the oxen for the burnt offerings, the threshing sledges for the wood, and the wheat for the grain offering. I will give all this.' But King David replied to Araunah, 'No, I insist on paying the full price. I will not take for the Lord what is yours, or sacrifice a burnt offering that costs me nothing.' So David paid Araunah six hundred shekels of gold for the site. David built an altar to the Lord there and sacrificed burnt offerings and fellowship offerings. He called on the Lord, and the Lord answered him with fire from heaven on the altar of burnt offering. Then the Lord spoke to the angel, and he put his sword back into its sheath" (1 Chr. 21:14-27).

Aaron Offers Sacrifices – "Then Aaron lifted his hands toward the people and blessed them. And having sacrificed the sin offering, the burnt offering and the fellowship offering, he stepped down. Moses and Aaron then went into the tent of meeting. When they came out, they blessed the people; and the glory of the Lord appeared to all the people. Fire came out from the presence of the Lord and consumed the burnt offering and the fat portions on the altar. And when all the people saw it, they shouted for joy and fell facedown" (Lev. 9:22-24).

Fire on the Sacrifices of Gideon – "Gideon went inside, prepared a young goat, and from an ephah of flour he made bread without yeast. Putting the meat in a basket and its broth in a pot, he brought them out and offered them to him under the oak. The angel of God said to him, 'Take the meat and the unleavened bread, place them on this rock, and pour out the broth.' And Gideon did so. Then the angel of the Lord touched the meat and the unleavened bread with the tip of the staff that was in his hand. Fire flared from the rock, consuming the meat and the bread. And the angel of the Lord disappeared. When Gideon realized that it was the angel of the Lord, he exclaimed, 'Alas, Sovereign Lord! I have seen the angel of the Lord face to face!' But the Lord said to him, 'Peace! Do not be afraid. You are not going to die.' So Gideon built an altar to the Lord there and called it The Lord Is Peace. To this day it stands in Ophrah of the Abiezrites" (Jdg. 6:19-24).

Fire on the Sacrifices of Manoah – "Manoah said to the angel of the Lord, 'We would like you to stay until we prepare a young goat for you.' The angel of the

Lord replied, 'Even though you detain me, I will not eat any of your food. But if you prepare a burnt offering, offer it to the Lord.' (Manoah did not realize that it was the angel of the Lord.) Then Manoah inquired of the angel of the Lord, 'What is your name, so that we may honor you when your word comes true?' He replied, 'Why do you ask my name? It is beyond understanding.' Then Manoah took a young goat, together with the grain offering, and sacrificed it on a rock to the Lord. And the Lord did an amazing thing while Manoah and his wife watched: As the flame blazed up from the altar toward heaven, the angel of the Lord ascended in the flame. Seeing this, Manoah and his wife fell with their faces to the ground" (Jdg. 13:15-20).

Fire on the Sacrifices of Solomon – "When Solomon finished praying, fire came down from heaven and consumed the burnt offering and the sacrifices, and the glory of the Lord filled the temple. The priests could not enter the temple of the Lord because the glory of the Lord filled it. When all the Israelites saw the fire coming down and the glory of the Lord above the temple, they knelt on the pavement with their faces to the ground, and they worshiped and gave thanks to the Lord, saying, 'He is good; His love endures forever'" (2 Chr. 7:1-3).

Fire on the Sacrifices of Elijah – "At the time of sacrifice, the prophet Elijah stepped forward and prayed: 'Lord, the God of Abraham, Isaac and Israel, let it be known today that you are God in Israel and that I am your servant and have done all these things at your command. Answer me, Lord, answer me, so these people will know that you, Lord, are God, and that you are turning their hearts back again.' Then the fire of the Lord fell and burned up the sacrifice, the wood, the stones and the soil, and also licked up the water in the trench. When all the people saw this, they fell prostrate and cried, 'The Lord—he is God! The Lord—he is God!' Then Elijah commanded them, 'Seize the prophets of Baal. Don't let anyone get away!' They seized them, and Elijah had them brought down to the Kishon Valley and slaughtered there" (1 Ki. 18:36-40).

Jeroboam Warned, Stricken – "By the word of the Lord a man of God came from Judah to Bethel, as Jeroboam was standing by the altar to make an offering. By the word of the Lord he cried out against the altar: 'Altar, altar! This is what the Lord says: A son named Josiah will be born to the house of David. On you he will sacrifice the priests of the high places who make offerings here, and human bones will be burned on you.' That same day the man of God gave a sign: 'This is the sign the Lord has declared: The altar will be split apart and the ashes on it will be poured out.' When King Jeroboam heard what the man of God cried out against the altar at Bethel, he stretched out his hand from the altar and said, 'Seize him!' But the hand he stretched out toward the man shriveled up, so that he could not pull it back. Also, the altar was split apart and its ashes poured out according to the sign given by the man of God by the word of the Lord. Then the king said to the man of God, 'Intercede with the Lord your God and pray for me that my hand may be restored.' So the man of God interceded with the Lord, and the king's hand was restored and became as it was before. The king said to the man of God, 'Come home with me for a meal, and I will give you a gift.' But the man of God answered the king, 'Even if you were to give me half your possessions, I would not go with you, nor would I eat bread or drink water here. For I was commanded by the word of the Lord: "You must not eat bread or drink water or return by the way you came.'" So he took another road and did not return by the way he had come to Bethel" (1 Ki. 13:1-10).

Provision for the Lepers – "Now there were four men with leprosy at the entrance of the city gate. They said to each other, 'Why stay here until we die? If we say, "We'll go into the city" — the famine is there, and we will die. And if we stay here, we will die. So let's go over to the camp of the Arameans and surrender. If they spare us, we live; if they kill us, then we die.' At dusk they got up and went to the camp of the Arameans. When they reached the edge of the camp, no one was there, for the Lord had caused the Arameans to hear the sound of chariots and horses and a great army, so that they said to one another, 'Look, the king of Israel has hired the Hittite and Egyptian kings to attack us!' So they got up and fled in the dusk and abandoned their tents and their horses and donkeys. They left the camp as it was and ran for their lives. The men who had leprosy reached the edge of the camp, entered one of the tents and ate and drank. Then they took silver, gold and clothes, and went off and hid them. They returned and entered another tent and took some things from it and hid them also" (2 Ki. 7:3-8).

Elijah Fed by Ravens – "Now Elijah the Tishbite, from Tishbe in Gilead, said to Ahab, 'As the Lord, the God of Israel, lives, whom I serve, there will be neither dew nor rain in the next few years except at my word.' Then the word of the Lord came to Elijah: 'Leave here, turn eastward and hide in the Kerith Ravine, east of the Jordan. You will drink from the brook, and I have directed the ravens to supply you with food there.' So he did what the Lord had told him. He went to the Kerith Ravine, east of the Jordan, and stayed there. The ravens brought him bread and meat in the morning and bread and meat in the evening, and he drank from the brook" (1 Ki. 17:1-6).

Elijah is Fed by an Angel – "Now Ahab told Jezebel everything Elijah had done and how he had killed all the prophets with the sword. So Jezebel sent a messenger to Elijah to say, 'May the gods deal with me, be it ever so severely, if by this time tomorrow I do not make your life like that of one of them.' Elijah was afraid and ran for his life. When he came to Beersheba in Judah, he left his servant there, while he himself went a day's journey into the wilderness. He came to a broom bush, sat down under it and prayed that he might die. 'I have had enough, Lord,' he said. 'Take my life; I am no better than my ancestors.' Then he lay down under the bush and fell asleep. All at once an angel touched him and said, 'Get up and eat.' He looked around, and there by his head was some bread baked over hot coals, and a jar of water. He ate and drank and then lay down again. The angel of the Lord came back a second time and touched him and said, 'Get up and eat, for the journey is too much for you.' So he got up and ate and drank. Strengthened by that food, he traveled forty days and forty nights until he reached Horeb, the mountain of God" (1 Ki. 19:1-8).

Meal and Oil Supplied to the Widow – "Then the word of the Lord came to him: 'Go at once to Zarephath in the region of Sidon and stay there. I have directed a widow there to supply you with food.' So he went to Zarephath. When he came to the town gate, a widow was there gathering sticks. He called to her and asked, 'Would you bring me a little water in a jar so I may have a drink?' As she was going to get it, he called, 'And bring me, please, a piece of bread.' 'As surely as the Lord your God lives,' she replied, 'I don't have any bread—only a handful of flour in a jar and a little olive oil in a jug. I am gathering a few sticks to take home and make a meal for myself and my son, that we may eat it—and die.' Elijah said to her, 'Don't be afraid. Go home and do as you have said. But first make a small loaf of bread for me from what you have and bring it to me, and then make something for yourself and your son. For this is what the Lord, the God of Israel, says: "The jar of flour will not be used up and the jug of oil will not run dry until the day the Lord sends rain on the land."' She went away and did as Elijah had told her. So there was food every day for Elijah and for the woman and her family. For the jar of flour was not used up and the jug of oil did not run dry, in keeping with the word of the Lord spoken by Elijah" (1 Ki. 17:8-16).

The Widow's Son is Raised – "Some time later the son of the woman who owned the house became ill. He grew worse and worse, and finally stopped breathing. She said to Elijah, 'What do you have against me, man of God? Did you come to remind me of my sin and kill my son?' 'Give me your son,' Elijah replied. He took him from her arms, carried him to the upper room where he was staying, and laid him on his bed. Then he cried out to the Lord, 'Lord my God, have you brought tragedy even on this widow I am staying with, by causing her son to die?' Then he stretched himself out on the boy three times and cried out to the Lord, 'Lord my God, let this boy's life return to him!' The Lord heard Elijah's cry, and the boy's life returned to him, and he lived. Elijah picked up the child and carried him down from the room into the house. He gave him to his mother and said, 'Look, your son is alive!' Then the woman said to Elijah, 'Now I know that you are a man of God and that the word of the Lord from your mouth is the truth'" (1 Ki. 17:17-24).

Rain after Elijah Prays – "And Elijah said to Ahab, 'Go, eat and drink, for there is the sound of a heavy rain.' So Ahab went off to eat and drink, but Elijah climbed to the top of Carmel, bent down to the ground and put his face between his knees. 'Go and look toward the sea,' he told his servant. And he went up and looked. 'There is nothing there,' he said. Seven times Elijah said, 'Go back.' The seventh time the servant reported, 'A cloud as small as a man's hand is rising from the sea.' So Elijah said, 'Go and tell Ahab, "Hitch up your chariot and go down before the rain stops you."' Meanwhile, the sky grew black with clouds, the wind rose, a heavy rain started falling and Ahab rode off to Jezreel. The power of the Lord came on Elijah and, tucking his cloak into his belt, he ran ahead of Ahab all the way to Jezreel" (1 Ki. 18:41-46).

Fire on Ahaziah's Army – "Then he sent to Elijah a captain with his company of fifty men. The captain went up to Elijah, who was sitting on the top of a hill, and said to him, 'Man of God, the king says, "Come down!"' Elijah answered the captain, 'If I am a man of God, may fire come down from heaven and consume you and your fifty men!' Then fire fell from heaven and consumed the captain and his men. At this the king sent to Elijah another captain with his fifty men. The captain said to him, 'Man of God, this is what the king says, "Come down at once!"' 'If I am a man of God,' Elijah replied, 'may fire come down from heaven and consume you and your fifty men!' Then the fire of God fell from heaven and consumed him and his fifty men" (2 Ki. 1:9-12).

The Jordan Divides - "Fifty men from the company of the prophets went and stood at a distance, facing the place where Elijah and Elisha had stopped at the Jordan. Elijah took his cloak, rolled it up and struck the water with it. The water divided to the right and to the left, and the two of them crossed over on dry ground" (2 Ki. 2:7-8).

Elijah's Translation – "When they had crossed, Elijah said to Elisha, 'Tell me, what can I do for you before I am taken from you?' 'Let me inherit a double portion of your spirit,' Elisha replied. 'You have asked a difficult thing,' Elijah said, 'yet if you see me when I am taken from you, it will be yours—otherwise, it will not.' As they were walking along and talking together, suddenly a chariot of fire and horses of fire appeared and separated the two of them, and Elijah went up to heaven in a whirlwind. Elisha saw this and cried out, 'My father! My father! The chariots and horsemen of Israel!' And Elisha saw him no more. Then he took hold of his garment and tore it in two. Elisha then picked up Elijah's cloak that had fallen from him and went back and stood on the bank of the Jordan. He took the cloak that had fallen from Elijah and struck the water with it. 'Where now is the Lord, the God of Elijah?' he asked. When he struck the water, it divided to the right and to the left, and he crossed over" (2 Ki. 2:9-14).

Waters of Jericho are Sweetened – "The people of the city said to Elisha, 'Look, our lord, this town is well situated, as you can see, but the water is bad and the land is unproductive.' 'Bring me a new bowl,' he said, 'and put salt in it.' So they brought it to him. Then he went out to the spring and threw the salt into it, saying, 'This is what the Lord says: "I have healed this water. Never again will it cause death or make the land unproductive."' And the water has remained pure to this day, according to the word Elisha had spoken" (2 Ki. 2:19-22).

Widow's Oil is Increased – "The wife of a man from the company of the prophets cried out to Elisha, 'Your servant my husband is dead, and you know that he revered the Lord. But now his creditor is coming to take my two boys as his slaves.' Elisha replied to her, 'How can I help you? Tell me, what do you have in your house?' 'Your servant has nothing there at all,' she said, 'except a small jar of olive oil.' Elisha said, 'Go around and ask all your neighbors for empty jars. Don't ask for just a few. Then go inside and shut the door behind you and your sons. Pour oil into all the jars, and as each is filled, put it to one side.' She left him and shut the door behind her and her sons. They brought the jars to her and she kept pouring. When all the jars were full, she said to her son, 'Bring me another one.' But he replied, 'There is not a jar left.' Then the oil stopped flowing. She went and told the man of God, and he said, 'Go, sell the oil and pay your debts. You and your sons can live on what is left'" (2 Ki. 4:1-7).

Shunammite's Child is Raised – "The child grew, and one day he went out to his father, who was with the reapers. He said to his father, 'My head! My head!' His father told a servant, 'Carry him to his mother.' After the servant had lifted him up and carried him to his mother, the boy sat on her lap until noon, and then he died. She went up and laid him on the bed of the man of God, then shut the door and went out. She called her husband and said, 'Please send me one of the servants and a donkey so I can go to the man of God quickly and return.' 'Why go to him today?' he asked. 'It's not the New Moon or the Sabbath.' 'That's all right,' she said. She saddled the donkey and said to her servant, 'Lead on; don't slow down for me unless I tell you.' So she set out and came to the man of God at Mount Carmel. When he saw her in the distance, the man of God said to his servant Gehazi, 'Look! There's the Shunammite! Run to meet her and ask her, "Are you all right? Is your husband all right? Is your child all right?"' 'Everything is all right,' she said. When she reached the man of God at the mountain, she took hold of his feet. Gehazi came over to push her away, but the man of God said, 'Leave her alone! She is in bitter distress, but the Lord has hidden it from me and has not told me why.' 'Did I ask you for a son, my lord?' she said. 'Didn't I tell you, "Don't raise my hopes"?' Elisha said to Gehazi, 'Tuck your cloak into your belt, take my staff in your hand and run. Don't greet anyone you meet, and if anyone greets you, do not answer. Lay my staff on the boy's face.' But the child's mother said, 'As surely as the Lord lives and as you live, I will not leave you.' So he got up and followed her. Gehazi went on ahead and laid the staff on the boy's face, but there was no sound or response. So Gehazi went back to meet Elisha and told him, 'The boy has not awakened.' When Elisha reached the house, there was the boy lying dead on his couch. He went in, shut the door on the two of them and prayed to the Lord. Then he got on the bed and lay on the boy, mouth to mouth, eyes to eyes, hands to hands. As he stretched himself out on him, the boy's body grew warm. Elisha turned away and walked back and forth in the room and then got on the bed and stretched out on him once more. The boy sneezed seven times and opened his eyes. Elisha summoned Gehazi and said, 'Call the Shunammite.' And he did. When she came, he said, 'Take your son.' She came in, fell at his feet and bowed to the ground. Then she took her son and went out" (2 Ki. 4:18-37).

The Poisonous Stew – "Elisha returned to Gilgal and there was a famine in that region. While the company of the prophets was meeting with him, he said to his servant, 'Put on the large pot and cook some stew for these prophets.' One of them went out into the fields to gather herbs and found a wild vine and picked as many of its gourds as his garment could hold. When he returned, he cut them up into the pot of stew, though no one knew what they were. The stew was poured out for the men, but as they began to eat it, they cried out, 'Man of God, there is death in the pot!' And they could not eat it. Elisha said, 'Get some flour.' He put it into the pot and said, 'Serve it to the people to eat.' And there was nothing harmful in the pot" (2 Ki. 4:38-41).

One Hundred Men Fed – "A man came from Baal Shalishah, bringing the man of God twenty loaves of barley bread baked from the first ripe grain, along with some heads of new grain. 'Give it to the people to eat,' Elisha said. 'How can I set this before a hundred men?'

his servant asked. But Elisha answered, 'Give it to the people to eat. For this is what the Lord says: 'They will eat and have some left over.'' Then he set it before them, and they ate and had some left over, according to the word of the Lord" (2 Ki. 4:42-44).

Naaman is Cursed – "Now Naaman, commander of the army of the king of Syria, was a great and honorable man in the eyes of his master, because by him the Lord had given victory to Syria. He was also a mighty man of valor, but a leper. And the Syrians had gone out on raids, and had brought back captive a young girl from the land of Israel. She waited on Naaman's wife. Then she said to her mistress, 'If only my master were with the prophet who is in Samaria! For he would heal him of his leprosy.' And Naaman went in and told his master, saying, 'Thus and thus said the girl who is from the land of Israel.' Then the king of Syria said, 'Go now, and I will send a letter to the king of Israel.' So he departed and took with him ten talents of silver, six thousand shekels of gold, and ten changes of clothing. Then he brought the letter to the king of Israel, which said, Now be advised, when this letter comes to you, that I have sent Naaman my servant to you, that you may heal him of his leprosy. And it happened, when the king of Israel read the letter, that he tore his clothes and said, 'Am I God, to kill and make alive, that this man sends a man to me to heal him of his leprosy? Therefore please consider, and see how he seeks a quarrel with me.' So it was, when Elisha the man of God heard that the king of Israel had torn his clothes, that he sent to the king, saying, 'Why have you torn your clothes? Please let him come to me, and he shall know that there is a prophet in Israel.' Then Naaman went with his horses and chariot, and he stood at the door of Elisha's house. And Elisha sent a messenger to him, saying, 'Go and wash in the Jordan seven times, and your flesh shall be restored to you, and you shall be clean.' But Naaman became furious, and went away and said, 'Indeed, I said to myself, 'He will surely come out to me, and stand and call on the name of the Lord his God, and wave his hand over the place, and heal the leprosy.' Are not the Abanah and the Pharpar, the rivers of Damascus, better than all the waters of Israel? Could I not wash in them and be clean?' So he turned and went away in a rage. And his servants came near and spoke to him, and said, 'My father, if the prophet had told you to do something great, would you not have done it? How much more then, when he says to you, "Wash, and be clean"?' So he went down and dipped seven times in the Jordan, according to the saying of the man of God; and his flesh was restored like the flesh of a little child, and he was clean. And he returned to the man of God, he and all his aides, and came and stood before him; and he said, "Indeed, now I know that there is no God in all the earth, except in Israel; now therefore, please take a gift from your servant." But he said, 'As the Lord lives, before whom I stand, I will receive nothing.' And he urged him to take it, but he refused. So Naaman said, 'Then, if not, please let your servant be given two mule-loads of earth; for your servant will no longer offer either burnt offering or sacrifice to other gods, but to the Lord. Yet in this thing may the Lord pardon your servant: when my master goes into the temple of Rimmon to worship there, and he leans on my hand, and I bow down in the temple of Rimmon—when I bow down in the temple of Rimmon, may the Lord please pardon your servant in this thing.' Then he said to him, 'Go in peace.' So he departed from him a short distance" (2 Ki. 5:1-19).[5]

Gehazi Stricken with Leprosy – "Then he said to him, 'Did not my heart go with you when the man turned back from his chariot to meet you? Is it time to receive money and to receive clothing, olive groves and vineyards, sheep and oxen, male and female servants? Therefore the leprosy of Naaman shall cling to you and your descendants forever.' And he went out from his presence leprous, as white as snow" (2 Ki. 5:26-27).

The Axhead Recovered – "And the sons of the prophets said to Elisha, 'See now, the place where we dwell with you is too small for us. Please, let us go to the Jordan, and let every man take a beam from there, and let us make there a place where we may dwell.' So he answered, 'Go.' Then one said, 'Please consent to go with your servants.' And he answered, 'I will go.' So he went with them. And when they came to the Jordan, they cut down trees. But as one was cutting down a tree, the iron ax head fell into the water; and he cried out and said, 'Alas, master! For it was borrowed.' So the man of God said, 'Where did it fall?' And he showed him the place. So he cut off a stick, and threw it in there; and he made the iron float. Therefore he said, 'Pick it up for yourself.' So he reached out his hand and took it" (2 Ki. 6:1-7).

Eyes are Opened – "And when the servant of the man of God arose early and went out, there was an army,

---

[5] All Scripture quotations from this point forward, unless otherwise noted, are from the *New King James Version*.

surrounding the city with horses and chariots. And his servant said to him, 'Alas, my master! What shall we do?' So he answered, 'Do not fear, for those who are with us are more than those who are with them.' And Elisha prayed, and said, 'Lord, I pray, open his eyes that he may see.' Then the Lord opened the eyes of the young man, and he saw. And behold, the mountain was full of horses and chariots of fire all around Elisha. So when the Syrians came down to him, Elisha prayed to the Lord, and said, 'Strike this people, I pray, with blindness.' And He struck them with blindness according to the word of Elisha. Now Elisha said to them, 'This is not the way, nor is this the city. Follow me, and I will bring you to the man whom you seek.' But he led them to Samaria" (2 Ki. 6:15-19).

The Dead Restored Back to life – "Then Elisha died, and they buried him. And the raiding bands from Moab invaded the land in the spring of the year. So it was, as they were burying a man, that suddenly they spied a band of raiders; and they put the man in the tomb of Elisha; and when the man was let down and touched the bones of Elisha, he revived and stood on his feet" (2 Ki. 13:20-21).

The Sun Dial – "And Hezekiah said to Isaiah, 'What is the sign that the Lord will heal me, and that I shall go up to the house of the Lord the third day?' Then Isaiah said, 'This is the sign to you from the Lord, that the Lord will do the thing which He has spoken: shall the shadow go forward ten degrees or go backward ten degrees?' And Hezekiah answered, 'It is an easy thing for the shadow to go down ten degrees; no, but let the shadow go backward ten degrees.' So Isaiah the prophet cried out to the Lord, and He brought the shadow ten degrees backward, by which it had gone down on the sundial of Ahaz" (2 Ki. 20:8-11).

Hezekiah Healed – "In those days Hezekiah was sick and near death. And Isaiah the prophet, the son of Amoz, went to him and said to him, Thus says the Lord: 'Set your house in order, for you shall die and not live.' Then Hezekiah turned his face toward the wall, and prayed to the Lord, and said, 'Remember now, O Lord, I pray, how I have walked before You in truth and with a loyal heart, and have done what is good in Your sight.' And Hezekiah wept bitterly. And the word of the Lord came to Isaiah, saying, 'Go and tell Hezekiah, 'Thus says the Lord, the God of David your father: 'I have heard your prayer, I have seen your tears; surely I will add to your days fifteen years. I will deliver you and this city from the hand of the king of Assyria, and I will defend this city.' And this is the sign to you from the Lord, that the Lord will do this thing which He has spoken: Behold, I will bring the shadow on the sundial, which has gone down with the sun on the sundial of Ahaz, ten degrees backward." So the sun returned ten degrees on the dial by which it had gone down. This is the writing of Hezekiah king of Judah, when he had been sick and had recovered from his sickness: I said, 'In the prime of my life I shall go to the gates of Sheol; I am deprived of the remainder of my years.' I said, 'I shall not see YAH, The Lord in the land of the living; I shall observe man no more among the inhabitants of the world. My life span is gone, taken from me like a shepherd's tent; I have cut off my life like a weaver. He cuts me off from the loom; From day until night You make an end of me. I have considered until morning—Like a lion, So He breaks all my bones; From day until night You make an end of me. Like a crane or a swallow, so I chattered; I mourned like a dove; My eyes fail from looking upward. O Lord, I am oppressed; Undertake for me! What shall I say? He has both spoken to me, And He Himself has done it. I shall walk carefully all my years In the bitterness of my soul. O Lord, by these things men live; And in all these things is the life of my spirit; so You will restore me and make me live. Indeed it was for my own peace That I had great bitterness; But You have lovingly delivered my soul from the pit of corruption, For You have cast all my sins behind Your back. For Sheol cannot thank You, Death cannot praise You; Those who go down to the pit cannot hope for Your truth. The living, the living man, he shall praise You, As I do this day; The father shall make known Your truth to the children. "The Lord was ready to save me; Therefore we will sing my songs with stringed instruments All the days of our life, in the house of the Lord." Now Isaiah had said, "Let them take a lump of figs, and apply it as a poultice on the boil, and he shall recover." And Hezekiah had said, 'What is the sign that I shall go up to the house of the Lord?'" (Is. 38).

Daniel's Friends Protected – "And these three men, Shadrach, Meshach, and Abed-Nego, fell down bound into the midst of the burning fiery furnace. Then King Nebuchadnezzar was astonished; and he rose in haste and spoke, saying to his counselors, 'Did we not cast three men bound into the midst of the fire?' They answered and said to the king, 'True, O king.' 'Look!' he answered, 'I see four men loose, walking in the midst of the fire; and they are not hurt, and the form of the fourth is like the Son of God.' Then Nebuchadnezzar went near the mouth of the burning fiery furnace and spoke, saying, 'Shadrach, Meshach, and Abed-Nego, servants of the Most High God, come out, and come here.' Then Shadrach, Meshach, and Abed-Nego came from the midst of the fire. And the satraps, administrators, governors, and the king's counselors gathered together, and they saw these men on whose bodies the fire had no power; the hair of their head was not singed nor were their garments affected, and the smell of fire was not on them" (Da. 3:23-27).

Deliverance of Daniel – "Then the king arose very early in the morning and went in haste to the den of lions. And when he came to the den, he cried out with a lamenting voice to Daniel. The king spoke, saying to Daniel, 'Daniel, servant of the living God, has your God, whom you serve continually, been able to deliver you from the lions?' Then Daniel said to the king, 'O king, live forever! My God sent His angel and shut the lions' mouths, so that they have not hurt me, because I was found innocent before Him; and also, O king, I have done no wrong before you.' Then the king was exceedingly glad for him, and commanded that they should take Daniel up out of the den. So Daniel was taken up out of the den, and no injury whatever was found on him, because he believed in his God. And the king gave the command, and they brought those men who had accused Daniel, and they cast them into the den of lions—them, their children, and their wives; and the lions overpowered them, and broke all their bones in pieces before they ever came to the bottom of the den" (Da. 6:19-24).

The Sea Calmed – "So they picked up Jonah and threw him into the sea, and the sea ceased from its raging.

Then the men feared the Lord exceedingly, and offered a sacrifice to the Lord and took vows" (Jon. 1:15-16).

Jonah Swallowed by Fish – "Now the Lord had prepared a great fish to swallow Jonah. And Jonah was in the belly of the fish three days and three nights" (Jon. 1:17).

Jonah Vomited by Fish - "Who can tell if God will turn and relent, and turn away from His fierce anger, so that we may not perish? Then God saw their works, that they turned from their evil way; and God relented from the disaster that He had said He would bring upon them, and He did not do it" (Jon. 2:9-10).

DAILY FAITH CONFESSIONS

(These are not direct quotations from the Bible but are paraphrased confessions based on scripture.)
SAY THEM OUT LOUD.

I am God's child (Jn. 1:12). I am royalty (1 Pet. 2:9). I am hidden with Christ in God (Col. 3:3). I am united with the Lord (1 Cor. 6:17). I am a friend of Christ (Jn. 15:15). I am raised up with Him, and seated with Him in heavenly places in Christ Jesus (Eph. 2:6). I was bought with a price (1 Cor. 6:19-20). I am blessed when I come in, and blessed shall I be when I go out (Deut. 28:6). I am a personal witness of Christ (Acts 1:8). I am a saint who prays in the Holy Spirit to keep myself in the love of God (Jude 1:20-21). I draw near with confidence to the throne of grace (Heb. 4:16). I have been adopted by the Father (Eph. 1:5). I am the salt and light of the earth (Mt. 5:13). I am the head and not the tail, and I am above, and not underneath. I am the lender and not the borrower (Deut. 28:13). I have authority to trample serpents and scorpions and over all the power of the enemy (Lk. 10:19). I am a member of the body of Christ (1 Cor. 12:27). God blessed me to be fruitful, and multiply, and replenish the earth, and subdue it: and have dominion (Gen. 1:28). I cannot be separated from God's love (Ro. 8:39). The good work God has begun in me will be perfected (Phil. 1:5). I can do all things through Christ who strengthens me (Phil. 4:13). No weapon that is formed against me will prosper (Is. 54:17). So then faith cometh by hearing, and hearing by the word of God (Ro. 10:17 KJV). Faith is my currency to operate in the kingdom of God (Ro. 14:23). I am God's workmanship created in Christ Jesus for good works, which God prepared beforehand (Eph. 2:10). I have been appointed to bear fruit, and that my fruit would remain (Jn. 15:16). I am being wise when I am winning souls for King Jesus (Pr. 11:30). My body is the temple of the Holy Spirit (1 Cor. 6:19). I have access to God through the Holy Spirit (Eph. 2:18). I have been justified (Ro. 5:1). Therefore there is now no condemnation for those who are in Christ Jesus (Ro. 8:1). Greater is He who is in me than he who is in the world (1 Jn. 4:4). I will do greater works than Jesus because He went to the Father (Jn. 14:12). As God was with Moses, He will be with me; God will not fail me or forsake me (Jos. 1:5). I see myself the way God see me. God sees me as a king (Gen, 17:6, Rev. 1:6) God sees me as royalty (1 Pet. 2:9). God sees me as the righteousness of God in Christ, bold as a lion (Ro. 3:22, Pr. 28:1). God sees me without spot or wrinkle because of the blood of Jesus (1 Pet. 1:19). I am having faith for big things because God owns everything and I'm His son (Ps. 24:1). No man will be able to stand before me all the days of my life (Jos. 1:5). My Father is glorified by this that I bear much fruit, and proves I'm a disciple (see Jn. 15:8). I think big and confess big things because God is big (Ps. 24:1). I will respect God for the big God that He is and my mouth will create whatever I want (Lk. 6:45). I no longer think of millions, my renewed mind thinks of billions because the wealth of the wicked is laid up for the righteous (Pr. 13:22). The sinner's job is to gather and collect for the one who is good in God's sight (Ecc. 2:26). Redemption is not complete without prosperity. Jesus hung on the cross so I can have the whole package, not just salvation (2 Cor. 8:9). I don't have to qualify, Jesus has qualified me. Jesus reversed the curse. The devil is a liar, and Jesus is the Messiah. Jesus is made unto me wisdom, righteousness, sanctification, and redemption (1 Cor. 1:30). I submit to God, I resist the devil and he flees from me (Jas. 4:7). For God has not given me the spirit of fear; but of power, and of love, and of a sound mind (2 Tim. 1:7). The Holy Spirit will teach me all things (Jn. 14:26). The Holy Spirit will guide me into all truth (Jn.16:13). The Holy Spirit abides in me, and I don't need anyone to teach me, but the anointing teaches me all things (1 Jn. 2:27). I quench fiery darts from the wicked one with the shield of faith (Eph. 6:16). I stand firm against the schemes of the devil (Eph. 6:11). I already have the victory and Satan cannot back me up. I advance and hold. Advance and hold to victory after victory (2 Cor. 2:14). I walk in love and live by faith (Gal. 5:6). I have been redeemed from the curse of the law, poverty, sickness, and spiritual death (Gal. 3:13; Deut. 28). I bear much fruit. I'm God's workmanship created beforehand for good works (Eph. 2:10). God's favor is on my life (Ps. 3:8). God blesses me and His favor surrounds me as with a shield (Ps. 5:12). The kingdom of God is within me (Lk. 17:21). I have a production plant inside of me that bears fruit to change the world (Gen. 1:28). God gives me power to get wealth to establish His covenant on earth (Deut. 8:18). I am blessed to be a blessing (Gen. 12:2). I have Satan on the run and will make a mockery of him (Jas. 4:7). No man will be able to stand before me all the days of my life (Jos. 1:5). God's angels keep me in all my ways (Ps. 91:11).

PRAYER FOR SALVATION

Say the following prayer out loud.

Heavenly Father, I am a sinner and I need a Savior. I confess Jesus Christ as the Lord of my life. I repent of all my sins. Father, I truly believe you raised Jesus from the dead. I pray this prayer in Jesus' name. Father, I am your child because Jesus is my Lord. I want to receive the fullness of the Holy Spirit. Holy Spirit come into me and fill me so I can be a mighty witness for King Jesus. I pray this prayer in Jesus' name. Amen.

PRAYER FOR BAPTISM OF THE HOLY SPIRIT

Say the following prayer out loud.

Father, I am your child because Jesus is my Lord. Jesus said, "How much more shall your heavenly Father give the Holy Spirit to those who ask Him." I ask you now in the name of Jesus to fill me with the Holy Spirit. Thank you, Father, I received the baptism of the Holy Spirit by faith. I yield my vocal organs and expect to speak in tongues as the Holy Spirit gives me utterance in Jesus name. Father, I plan to pray in the Holy Spirit building myself up on my most holy faith, and keep myself in the love of God, as mentioned in Jude 20 and 21. In Jesus name I decree it. Amen.

ABOUT THE AUTHOR

Eugene Carvalho is an administrator, Christian author of one hundred twenty books, and the founder of Receiving by Faith. God uses him in the offices of pastor, evangelist and prophet. He holds a bachelor's degree in biblical studies and a double minor in pastoral ministry and world missions. He also holds a master's degree in practical theology. Eugene prayed for a translator and God sent his wife Mercedes who has a six-year degree in Spanish from a university in Tampico, Mexico. They have participated in evangelism in the streets of Mexico for many years. They have also traveled to churches all over the United States and the nation of Mexico winning souls and preaching the gospel of the kingdom. Their website for their ministry is: www.receivingbyfaith.org.

BOOKS BY EUGENE IN ENGLISH

For a complete list of other books by Eugene visit receivingbyfaith.org or amazon.com.

Receiving by Faith
Faith for Every Day: 365 Daily Devotions
Faith Cometh by Hearing, and Hearing by the Word of God
Faith, Hope, and Love
Walk in Love and Live by Faith
Topical Christian Handbook and Scripture Guide
The Gospel Is the Power of God unto Salvation
Seed Time and Harvest Time
Your New Identity in Christ
The Cross and the Blood
The Holy Spirit
The Attributes of God
The Favor of God
The Glory of God
The Grace of God
The Power of God
The Promises of God
The Spirit of God
The Throne of God
The New Testament Church: A Survey from the Book of Ephesians
Vengeance and Recompense
God's Angel's
Prayer and Fasting
God's Mighty Prophets
A Survey of Jesus Through the Epistles

Old Testament Miracles
New Testament Miracles
The Fear of the Lord Is the Beginning of Knowledge; Fools Despise Wisdom and Instruction
The Psalms of David
Faith Without Works Is Dead
The Names of Jesus
Mountain Moving Confessions
In Him Was Life; and the Life Was the Light of Men
Visions and Dreams
Having Shod Your Feet with the Preparation of the Gospel of Peace
Blessed Beyond Measure
The Righteous Will Flourish like The Palm Tree
Christ Heals: What the Bible Has to Say
Jesus Is the Way, and the Truth, and the Life
My Peace I Give to You
Balancing Grace and Truth
The Old and New Testament Supernatural Acts of God Almighty
Praise and Worship Changes Everything
Understanding the Importance of Authority
If You Are Willing and Obedient
Have Faith in Jesus and the Finished Work of the Cross
Have Life More Abundantly
Pray in the Holy Spirit; Guard and Keep Yourselves in the Love of God
Sing Unto the Lord a New Song
The Power of the Tongue

You Have Authority and Power: Take Back What the Devil Stole

Be Strong and Courageous

Prayer and Praise: The Big Artillery

Apostles and Prophets: The Foundation of the Church

Covenant: A Concise Survey

Sow Then Reap a Harvest

God Has Not Given Us a Spirit of Timidity, But of Power, Love, and Discipline

Blessed and Highly Favored

Grace and Peace Be Multiplied Unto You

Your Word Is a Lamp to Me Feet

John: A Key Word Study Made Simple

For Momentary, Light Affliction Is Producing For Us an Eternal Weight of Glory

Prayer Is Powerful: What the Bible Has to Say

My People Are Destroyed By Lack of Knowledge

God Deserves Pure Worship

The Mouth of the Righteous is a Fountain of Life

The Lord Requires Integrity: The Major Element of Leadership

Weeping May Last for the Night, But a Shout of Joy Comes in the Morning

A Topical Look at the Book of Deuteronomy

A Topical Look at the Book of Psalms

A Topical Look at the Book of Proverbs

A Topical Look at the Book of Isaiah

A Topical Look at the Book of John

A Topical Look at the Book of Hebrews

A Topical Look at the Book of Revelation

BOOKS BY EUGENE IN SPANISH

Las Promesas de Dios
Los Salmos de David
Lo Sobrenatural: Lo que la Bíblia Tiene que Decir
Una Mirada Topica Del Libro De Los Salmos
Dios es Amor: Lo que la Biblia Tiene que Decir
La Adquisición de la Sabiduría es Vital: Lo que la
Biblia Tiene que Decir

NOTES

NOTES

NOTES